Glen Coe

Colin Baxter Photography, Grantown-on-Spey, Scotland

Glen Coe

Glen Coe is one of the most famous glens in Scotland, both for the bloody story of the infamous Massacre of Glencoe in 1692 and for its spectacular scenery. Glen Coe's steep rocky peaks rise high above its narrow valley, which runs for 13km, from the edge of Rannoch Moor below the great peak of Buachaille Etive Mòr to the sea at Loch Leven. The classic view is looking down the glen from where it narrows at 'The Study' where three huge buttresses, the Three Sisters of Glen Coe, dominate the view. These were formed by the glaciers that ground out the deep glen, and chopped off the ends of the spurs to leave these big cliffs. Whilst ice influenced the shape of the scenery, the type of rock makes a difference here too. Glen Coe is the remnant of a massive ancient volcano. The granite and rhyolite rocks formed by this volcanic activity are hard and form dramatic cliffs. Fire and ice, volcanoes and glaciers, carved the glen and the mountains to create the splendid landscape that it is today.

A main road – the A82 – runs through Glen Coe, making it easily accessible. Glencoe village lies at the foot of the glen, the King's House Hotel at its head. In the lower glen there are campsites, a youth hostel and the Clachaig Inn. There is also an interesting environmentally friendly National Trust for Scotland Visitor Centre, with café and shop, that is worth a few hours of time. Glen Coe has been owned by the National Trust for Scotland since 1935.

The mountains of Glen Coe are some of the most impressive and beautiful in Scotland. This book describes eight hill walks over seventeen of the finest hills, in Glen Coe, neighbouring Glen Etive and the Black Mount, all of them Munros. These are rough, rugged, spectacular walks, every one a gem.

To Fort William
Loch Linnhe
Loch Leven
South Ballachulish
Invercoe
Glencoe
Sgòrr na Ciche 740
Meall Dearg 953
Sgòr nam Fiannaidh 967
Aonach Eagach
Ballachulish
Creag Ghorm
A828
Kentallen
To Oban
Sgòrr Dhonuill 1001
Sgòrr Dhearg 1024
Beinn a' Bheithir
Visitor Centre
Clachaig Inn
Glen Coe
Loch Achtriochtan
River Coe
A82
Meall Mòr 676
Stob Coire nan Lochan
Gearr Aonach
Beinn Fhada 811
Bidean nam Bian 1150
1072
934
Buachaille Etive Beag 925
Stob Dubh 958
Buachaille Etive Mor
Stob Dearg 1022
956 Stob na Bròige
River Coupall
Sròn a' Choire Odhair
Beinn Bheag
Blackwater Reservoir
707 Meall a' Bhalach
Beinn a' Chrùlaiste 857
King's House Hotel
Gleann Duror
River Laroch
Gleann an Fhiodh
Creag Bhàn
772
Fionn Ghleann
Beinn Maol Chaluim 907
Allt Fhaolain
Sgor na h-Ulaidh 994
Fraochaidh 879
Corbhainn
Salachail
Dalness
Alltchaorann
Glen Etive
River Etive
Sron na Creise 900
Cam Ghleann
Glencoe Ski area
Creise
1108 Meall a' Bhùiridh
Beinn Mhic Chasgaig 864
1098 Clach Leathad
Glen Creran
River Creran
Beinn Mhic na Cèisich
758 Meall a' Bhuiridh
Beinn Fhionnlaidh 959
Allt Chaorach
Beinn Ceitlein
Allt a' Chaorainn
Allt Coire Ghiubhasan
Aonach Mòr
Elleric
Fasnacloich
Invercreran
Loch Baile Mhic Chailein
Glen Ure
River Ure
684 Stob Gaibhre
937
813 Beinn Sgulaird
Inverchamnan
Glenceitlein
Allt nan Gaoirean
Allt Ceitlein
Black Mount
River Bà
Glenetive Ho.
Coileitir
Gualachulain
Kinlochetive
Stob a' Bhruaich Leith 940
Stob a' Choire Odhair 945
1090 Stob Ghabhar
928 Meall nan Eun
Stob Coir' an Albannaich 1044
Beinn Trilleachan 839
Loch Etive
Ben Starav 1078
Glas Bheinn Mhòr 997
Beinn nan Aighenan 960
Loch Dochard
Forest Lodge
Blackmount
A road
B road
Minor road
Track
Classic route
Munro
0 5 kilometres
0 3 miles
N

	Route Name	Distance	Ascent	Time	Difficulty
1	The Aonach Eagach over ***Meall Dearg*** and ***Sgòrr nam Fiannaidh***	*16km (10 miles)*	*1285m (4130ft)*	*4–6 hours*	★★★★
2	Beinn a'Bheithir from Ballachulish over ***Sgòrr Dhonuill*** and ***Sgòrr Dhearg***	*15km (9.5 miles)*	*1400m (4500ft)*	*5–7 hours*	★★
3	***Bidean nam Bian*** and ***Stob Coire Sgrèamhach***	*11km (7 miles)*	*1400m (4500ft)*	*5–7 hours*	★★
4	Buachaille Etive Beag from Glen Coe over ***Stob Coire Raineach*** & ***Stob Dubh***	*12km (7.5 miles)*	*985m (3166ft)*	*4–5 hours*	★
5	Buachaille Etive Mòr: ***Stob Dearg*** and ***Stob na Bròige***	*14km (8.5 miles)*	*1250m (4017ft)*	*6–8 hours*	★★
6	The Northern Black Mount: ***Creise*** and ***Meall a'Bhùiridh***	*10km (6 miles)*	*1100m (3535ft)*	*5–6 hours*	★★
7	The Southern Black Mount: ***Stob Ghabhar*** and ***Stob a' Choire Odhair***	*16km (10 miles)*	*1275m (4098ft)*	*6–8 hours*	★★
8	***Ben Starav***, ***Beinn nan Aighenan*** and ***Glas Bheinn Mhòr*** from Glen Etive	*19.5km (12 miles)*	*2000m (6428ft)*	*8–10 hours*	★★★

Sgòr nam Fiannaidh 967
Aonach Eagach
Meall Garbh 939
Meall Dearg 953
873
Am Bodach
The Chancellor
Glen Coe
A' Chailleach
Sròn a' Choire Odhair Bhig
Allt a' Choire Odhair-bhig
706 Stob Mhic Mhartuin
Devil's Staircase
Beinn Bheag
Lochan na Fèithe
0 2 kilometres
0 1 miles
N
Clachaig Inn
Achnambeithach
Loch Achtriochtan
River Coe
Alt na reigh
To Fort William
Meeting of Three Waters
A82
Altnafeadh
636 Stob Beinn a' Chrùlaiste
857 Beinn a' Chrùlaiste
Lagangarbh
Lochan na Fola
Aonach Dubh
The Three Sisters
Gearr Aonach
Allt Coire Gabhail
Beinn Fhada
811
Stob nan Cabar 776
Buachaille Etive Beag
925 Stob Coire Raineach
River Coupall
To Crianlarich
An t-Sròn
1115 Stob Coire nan Lochan
931
Allt Lairig Eilde
Lairig Gartain
Stob Dearg 1022
Bidean nam Bian
1150
Stob Coire Sgrèamhach 1072
Stob Dubh 958
Buachaille Etive Mòr
Glen Etive
Allt Cam Ghlinne
Gleann Fhaolain
Allt Fhaolain
778
Bealach Fhionnghaill 907
Beinn Maol Chaluim
846
Stob na Bròige 956
Allt Gartain
River Etive
900 Sron na Creise
Allt Fionn Ghlinne
Dalness
Alltchaorann
Creise 1100

Walking in Glen Coe

The Glen Coe hills are steep and rocky, rising abruptly from narrow glens. The area is very accessible and long walk-ins are not usually required. In fact distances are quite short, often less than 16km (10mi). However the amount of ascent is high for most hills, usually well over 1000m (3000ft), so walks involve steep climbs and descents. Generally these climbs are on clear paths, though these are often rough, rocky and narrow, and sometimes exposed to big drops. On some routes, especially the Aonach Eagach, scrambling is required and there is great exposure. As a contrast to this, some mountains have long broad summit ridges making for easy walking, examples being Buachaille Etive Mòr and Beinn a'Bheithir. Overall though, climbing the Glen Coe hills is a strenuous and challenging activity. The rewards are a feeling of being amongst big, impressive mountains with dramatic rock scenery. The hills here are all different and there is no such thing as a typical Glen Coe day. Indeed, the huge variety of landscapes found in the region is one of the great joys of Glen Coe. A day may start with an easy approach over gentle moorland towards a massive peak (Buachaille Etive Mòr, the Southern Black Mount) or abruptly with an ascent up a steep, narrow corrie or stony hillside (Aonach Eagach, Bidean nam Bian). Once on the mountain, steep climbs lead up wild corries or along rocky ridges to the summits, and in clear weather there are views of tightly packed mountains split by deep glens, and out to the west, a seascape of lochs, islands and hills. When mist shrouds the summits the walking is mysterious and exciting. Rocks loom up like giant peaks only to dwindle as you draw close. The clouds rise and fall, sometime splitting open to reveal sudden views into the depths below. Glen Coe is a wonderful experience whatever the weather.

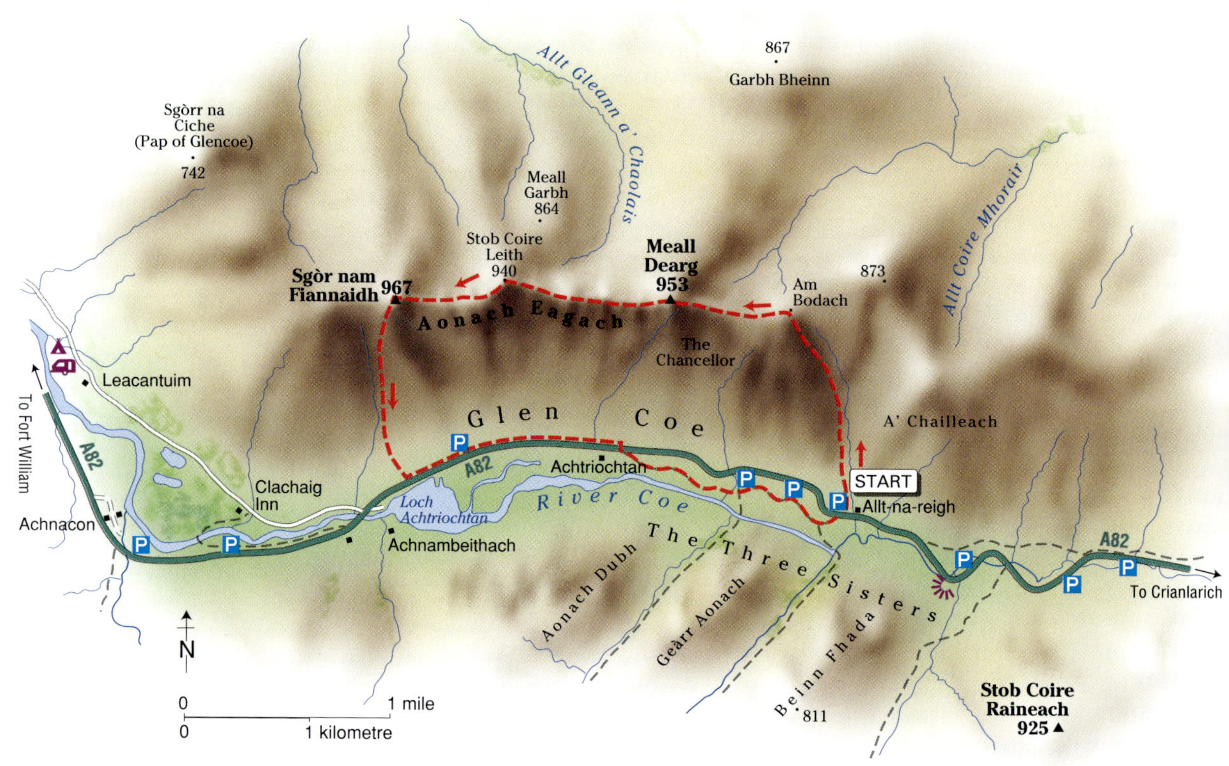

867
Garbh Bheinn
Allt Gleann a' Chaolais
Sgòrr na Ciche (Pap of Glencoe)
742
Meall Garbh 864
Stob Coire Leith 940
Meall Dearg 953
Sgòr nam Fiannaidh 967
Am Bodach
873
Allt Coire Mhorair
Aonach Eagach
The Chancellor
Leacantuim
To Fort William
A82
Glen Coe
A' Chailleach
START
Achtriochtan
Clachaig Inn
Achnacon
Loch Achtriochtan
River Coe
Allt-na-reigh
Achnambeithach
The Three Sisters
Aonach Dubh
Gearr Aonach
Beinn Fhada
811
Stob Coire Raineach 925
To Crianlarich
N
0
1 mile
0
1 kilometre

1. The Aonach Eagach

The steep slopes and jagged crest of the Aonach Eagach (the notched ridge) dominates the north side of Glen Coe, an intimidating mountain wall rising abruptly from the narrow glen. There are two Munros on the ridge – 953m Meall Dearg (red hill) and 967m Sgòrr nam Fiannaidh (peak of the Fingalians) – separated by a twisting arête of rock pinnacles and buttresses. The traverse of the Aonach Eagach is one of the great scrambles of the Scottish Highlands, a thrilling excursion into a world of steep rock. It's not difficult but it is exposed and a good head for heights is needed.

The two Munros can be climbed in separate outings from either end of the ridge but omitting the crest between them is to miss the best of the Aonach Eagach. There are splendid views from the ridge, especially across Glen Coe to massive Bidean nam Bian. The route is committing as there is no safe way down into Glen Coe between Meall Dearg at the east

The Aonach Eagach is a long scramble along a narrow rocky ridge. A good head for heights is needed. In winter this is a serious mountaineering expedition. There is no safe way down into Glen Coe from the ridge except at either end so this is a committing route.

THE AONACH EAGACH:

Meall Dearg *(212), 953m/3127ft. myowl d-yerrack; red hill*

Sgòrr nam Fiannaidh *(188), 967m/3173ft. sgor nam feeanee; peak of the fingalians*

Start/Finish *Allt-na-reigh, Glen Coe*

Distance
16km (10 miles)

Ascent
1285m (4130ft)

Time *4–6 hours*

Difficulty ★★★★

Maps *Harvey British Mountain Map Ben Nevis & Glen Coe, Harvey Superwalker Glen Coe, OS Explorer 384, OS Landranger 41*

Public Transport *Scottish Citylink buses run through Glen Coe*

Facilities *The Clachaig Inn, Glen Coe NTS Visitor Centre, Glencoe village*

Aonach Eagach and Glen Coe from Coire nam Beith. The Aonach Eagach is famous in Munro history, as the Rev. A.E. Robertson completed the first ever round of all the Munros on Meall Dearg in 1901.

end and Stob Coire Leith at the west end. East to west is the easiest way to traverse the Aonach Eagach, with a walk back up Glen Coe at the finish.

Start at the car park west of Allt-na-reigh where a signpost indicates the steep path up the shoulder of the subsidiary summit of Am Bodach (old man). The path soon reaches a stream called the Allt Ruigh and follows this upwards, with one big zigzag to avoid a deep gorge. After the stream disappears the path continues on to the ridge not far above. Turn west (left) here and climb a steep, stony slope to the summit of Am Bodach.

Descend just north of west from Am Bodach, where you encounter some steep, polished ledges. Climb down these with care, especially when they are wet, as there are steep drops below. Below the ledges the going is easier and a path leads along the narrow crest to Meall Dearg. The view is tremendous with the serrated narrow arête winding away to the west. The scramble along the ridge is exciting – round pinnacles, up gullies, across slabs. There are narrow paths below the rocks in places, avoiding the scrambling, but these are often more exposed and without any handholds. At the west end of the arête, just before the ascent to Stob Coire Leith (peak of the grey corrie), lies the hardest part of the traverse, a series of overhanging rock turrets, known as the Crazy Pinnacles, followed by a steep descent into a narrow notch and a steep climb up the far side. Once the pinnacles and notch have been negotiated the scrambling is over and it is an easy walk up broad slopes to Stob Coire Leith and on to Sgòrr nam Fiannaidh.

Looking west from Am Bodach along the Aonach Eagach. This narrow and challenging ridge was formed by glaciers that cut into the mountain on either side.

To descend back to Glen Coe head directly south down the steep hillside, which is rocky at the top and grassy lower down, with bits of path in places. Once down it's a 3km walk up the glen to Allt-na-reigh. The old road can be taken for much of the way.

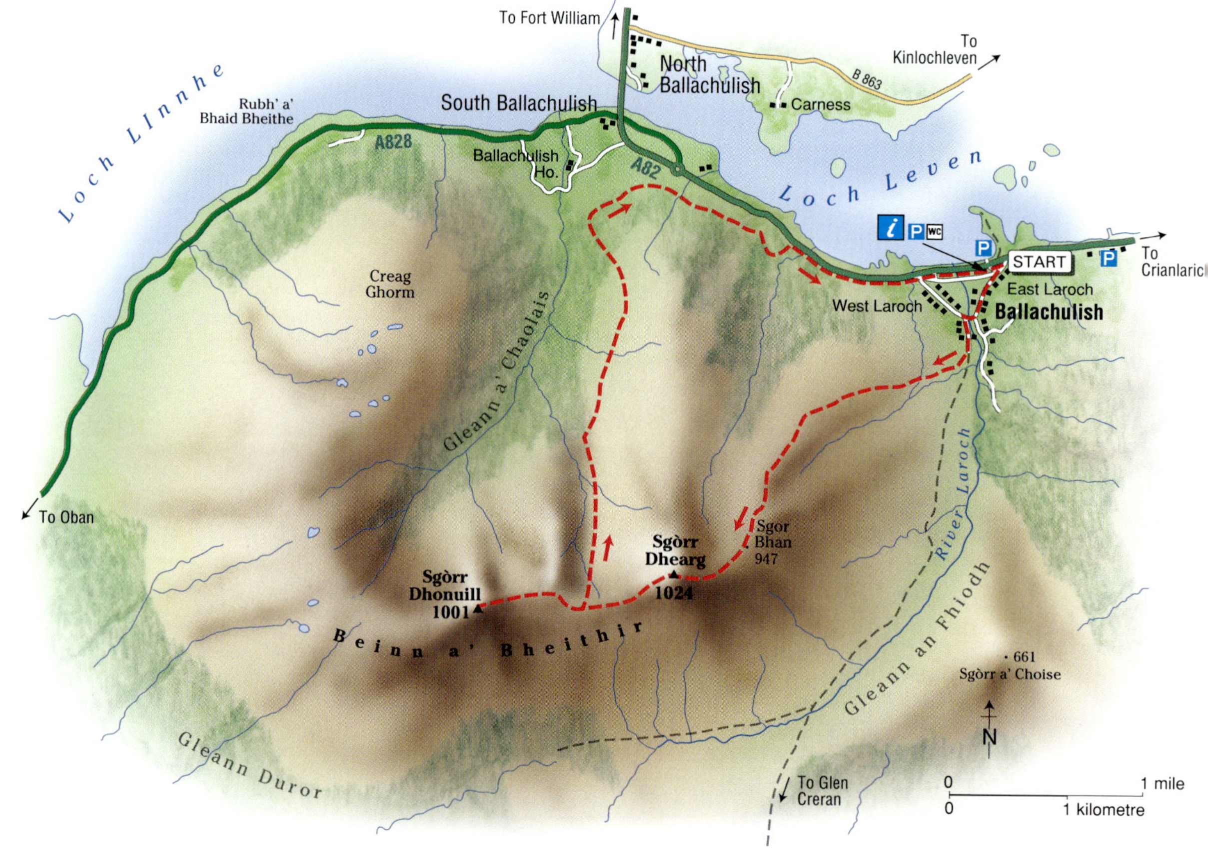

To Fort William
North Ballachulish
To Kinlochleven
B 863
Carness
Loch Linnhe
Rubh' a' Bhaid Bheithe
South Ballachulish
A828
Ballachulish Ho.
A82
Loch Leven
START
East Laroch
West Laroch
Ballachulish
To Crianlaric
Creag Ghorm
Gleann a' Chaolais
To Oban
Sgòrr Dhearg 1024
Sgor Bhan 947
Sgòrr Dhonuill 1001
Beinn a' Bheithir
River Laroch
Gleann an Fhiodh
661 Sgòrr a' Choise
N
Gleann Duror
To Glen Creran
0
1 mile
0
1 kilometre

2. Beinn a'Bheithir

Beinn a'Bheithir (hill of the demon or thunderbolt) is a graceful curving mountain rising above western Loch Leven to the west of Glen Coe. It looks superb from the Ballachulish Bridge. The two highest summits are both Munros – 1001m Sgòrr Dhonuill (Donald's peak) and 1024m Sgòrr Dhearg (red peak). The walking is easy with spacious views of the western seaboard and the mountains of Lochaber and Glen Coe. Beinn a'Bheithir sends long ridges down to the north with big forest-filled corries between them. The Forestry Commission has built 'mountain access' paths through Glenachulish Forest that make it practicable to venture into the dark confines of the conifers. The FC is also redesigning the forest to make it more open with a wider variety of trees, which will make it more attractive to walkers. Note that the mountain access paths were built from 2004-2005 and are not marked on older maps. To the north-east of Beinn a'Bheithir lies the old slate mining village of

A fine walk with a mixture of forest and open hillside. Some boggy sections. Steep in places. No continuous path. Superb views of sea lochs and mountains.

BEINN A' BHEITHIR:

Sgòrr Dhearg
(107), 1024m/3360ft
sgor d-yerrack;
red peak

Sgòrr Dhonuill
(137), 1001m/3284ft
sgor ghawil;
Donald's peak

Start/Finish
Ballachulish Information Centre

Distance
15km (9.5 miles)

Ascent
1400m (4500ft)

Time *5–7 hours*

Difficulty ★★

Maps *Harvey British Mountain Map Ben Nevis & Glen Coe, Harvey Superwalker Glen Coe, OS Explorer 384, OS Landranger 41*

Public Transport
Scottish Citylink and Highland buses run to Ballachulish from Edinburgh, Glasgow & Fort William

Facilities
Ballachulish, South Ballachulish

Looking east towards Sgòrr Dhonuill from Sgòrr Dhearg, Beinn a'Bheithir.

Ballachulish and it's here that the walk starts, at the Information Centre. Head south through Ballachulish for 0.5km then west to a bridge over the river Laroch. Cross the bridge to a signpost for the public footpath to Glen Creran. Turn left here and follow a minor road south past a church and the village primary school. Once past the latter turn right through a gate and climb westwards up grass and heather-clad slopes to a wide ridge where a path continues south-west to the subsidiary summit of Sgòr Bhan (white peak). As you climb this path ahead you can see the steeper, rockier north-east ridge, an alternative route that involves some easy scrambling.

From the tiny summit of Sgòr Bhan the rough path continues along the attractive narrow arête that curves elegantly round to Sgòrr Dhearg, a pale peak built of pink quartzite. Ahead a broad stony ridge runs west-south-west down to a saddle at 757m with Sgòrr Dhonuill's narrower east ridge rising beyond it. Sgòrr Dhonuill is made of dark granite and looks more sombre than Sgòrr Dhearg. A rough path leads down to the saddle and up the steep rocky ridge to Sgòrr Dhonuill. This, the lower of the two Munros is the better viewpoint, especially to the west where the rugged hills of Ardgour and Morvern rise above long fjord-like Loch Linnhe, which runs south-west to the Firth of Lorn and the distinctive summits of Ben More on Mull and the Paps of Jura. To the north Ben Nevis rises above the Mamores.

Return to the 757m saddle from Sgòrr Dhonuill and descend north down an initially steep and rocky path into boggy Gleann a'Chaolais heading for the Forestry Commission boundary fence and the start of a mountain access path that slants down through the forest. A line of fence posts runs beside the path. Follow the posts east round the top of the forest to where they start to climb away from the trees. Don't descend the centre of the corrie to the old path through the trees, a steep, muddy horror. The new path continues to contour along the edge of the forest before dropping down into the forest where it crosses a fence and zigzags down a grassy rake. It then crosses two forest roads and becomes an old forest road that descends to meet the main forest road just above a bridge. Turn away from the bridge and follow the road as it curves south-east down to the A82 road at St John's Church. Turn right here for the final section back to the start, a distance of a little under 2km.

Sgòrr Dhearg from Sgòrr Dhonuill. Beinn a'Bheithir was believed to be the home of the 'Cailleach Bheithir', Celtic goddess of storms, winter and darkness.

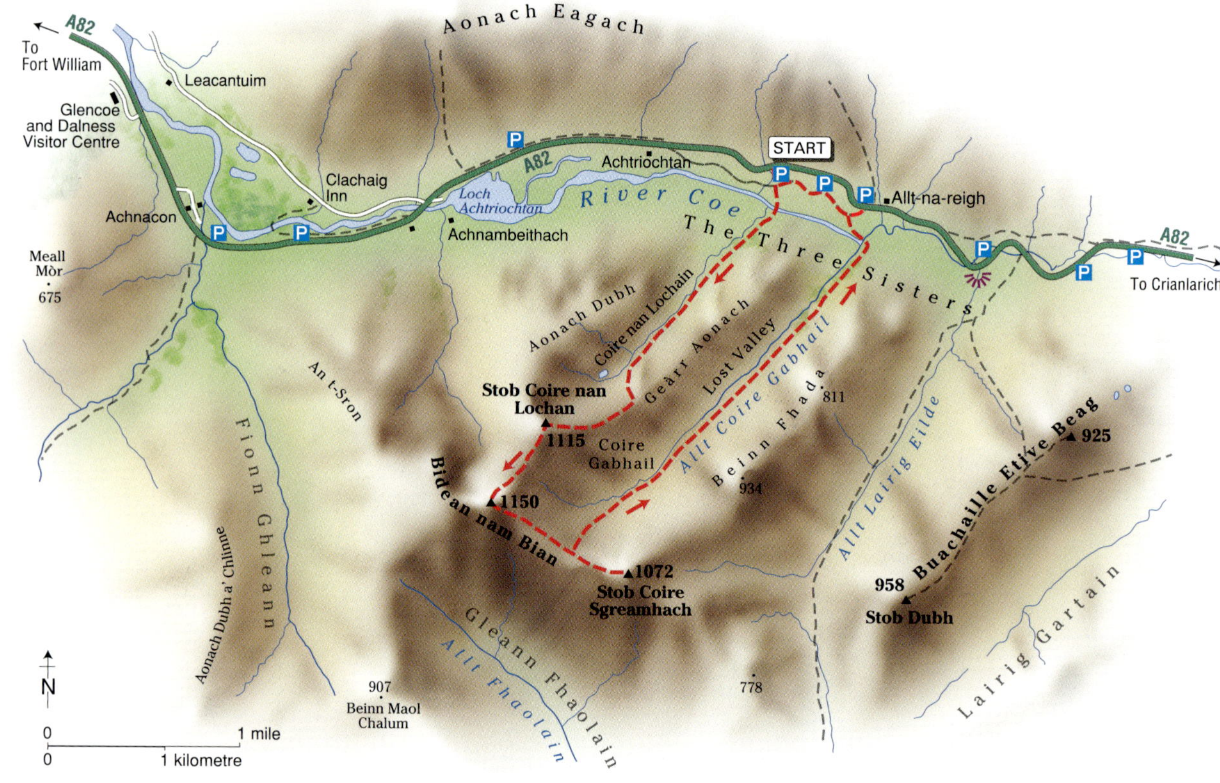

A82
To Fort William
Aonach Eagach
Leacantuim
Glencoe and Dalness Visitor Centre
Clachaig Inn
Achnacon
Loch Achtriochtan
Achtriochtan
START
Allt-na-reigh
River Coe
Achnambeithach
The Three Sisters
To Crianlarich
Meall Mòr
675
Aonach Dubh
Coire nan Lochain
Gearr Aonach
Lost Valley
Allt Coire Gabhail
An t-Sron
Stob Coire nan Lochan
1115
Coire Gabhail
Beinn Fhada
811
934
Allt Lairig Eilde
Buachaille Etive Beag
925
Bidean nam Bian
1150
1072
Stob Coire Sgreamhach
958
Stob Dubh
Fionn Ghleann
Aonach Dubh a' Chlinne
Gleann Fhaolain
Allt Fhaolain
Lairig Gartain
907
Beinn Maol Chalum
778
N
0
1 mile
0
1 kilometre

3. Bidean nam Bian & Stob Coire Sgrèamhach

Bidean nam Bian is a rugged and complex mountain massif and the highest peak in the Glen Coe area. There are two Munros – 1150m Bidean nam Bian itself, whose name possibly means peak of the mountains, and 1072m Stob Coire Sgrèamhach (peak of the dreadful corrie). Three long spurs ending in steep cliffs run down to Glen Coe from Bidean nam Bian, the famous Three Sisters of Glen Coe. These are, from west to east, Aonach Dubh (dark ridge), Gearr Aonach (short ridge) and Beinn Fhada (long hill).

To climb both Munros in one outing makes for a serious expedition involving steep, rocky slopes and potentially complex navigation. It's also arguably the finest walk in Glen Coe. The walk begins at the large car park in the heart of Glen Coe, half a km west of Allt-an-reigh, where a path runs down to a bridge across the River Coe then continues up into narrow Coire nan Lochain between Aonach Dubh and Gearr

A rugged walk over the highest and finest mountain in Glen Coe. The rocky terrain is complex and good navigation is required.

Bidean nam Bian *(23), 1150m/3773ft beetyan nam beeoan; peak of the mountains*

Stob Coire Sgrèamhach *(65), 1072m/3517ft stop korra skree-yach; peak of the dreadful corrie*

Start/Finish *Achnam-beithach, Glen Coe*

Distance *11km (7 miles)*

Ascent *1400m (4500ft)*

Time *5–7 hours*

Difficulty ★★

Maps *Harvey British Mountain Map Ben Nevis & Glen Coe, Harvey Superwalker Glen Coe, OS Explorer 384, OS Landranger 41*

Public Transport *Scottish Citylink buses run through Glen Coe*

Facilities *The Clachaig Inn, Glen Coe NTS Visitor Centre, Glencoe village*

Aonach, a spectacular place with big cliffs rising either side. The path runs beside the stream draining the corrie before fading away below steep slopes down which the stream crashes in a fine waterfall. You can scramble up the slopes close to the waterfall but it's easier to head left (south) and climb less rocky slopes into the open upper corrie. Turn left again here, heading south-east, and climb to the broad ridge of Gearr Aonach, which is then followed south and west up to the subsidiary peak of Stob Coire nan Lochain (peak of the corrie of the pool).

The last section to the summit is steep and rocky. Less than a km to the south-west lies Bidean nam Bian. Descend some 120m to a saddle then ascend a narrow rocky ridge to the tiny summit and a wonderful view of rugged mountains on all sides. Now on the main ridge of the mountain descend stony slopes south-east to a saddle at the head of Coire Gabhail then continue up the rocky ridge to Stob Coire

Sgrèamhach. The dramatic name of this peak presumably refers to Coire Gabhail (corrie of booty – a reference to its use as a hiding place for stolen cattle). The views back to Bidean nam Bian from Stob Coire Sgrèamhach are excellent.

The summit ridge of Bidean nam Bian, looking south-east.

Return to the saddle at the head of Coire Gabhail and look out for a small cairn that marks the start of the descent into the corrie. An eroded path runs down into a boulder field and then to the wide, flat, grass and shingle floor of the corrie. This is a lovely, restful spot after all the steep rough slopes. However the rough walking is not over yet. Because it's hidden from the road this is often known as the Lost Valley. What hides it is a steep ravine. The foot of the corrie is marked by some huge boulders. Pass these and then take the path on the east side of the spectacular ravine. The path descends steeply through wooded rocky slopes to ease at an area of forest regeneration beyond which is a bridge over the River Coe and a short ascent back to the start.

Stob Coire nan Lochain from the north-east (left).

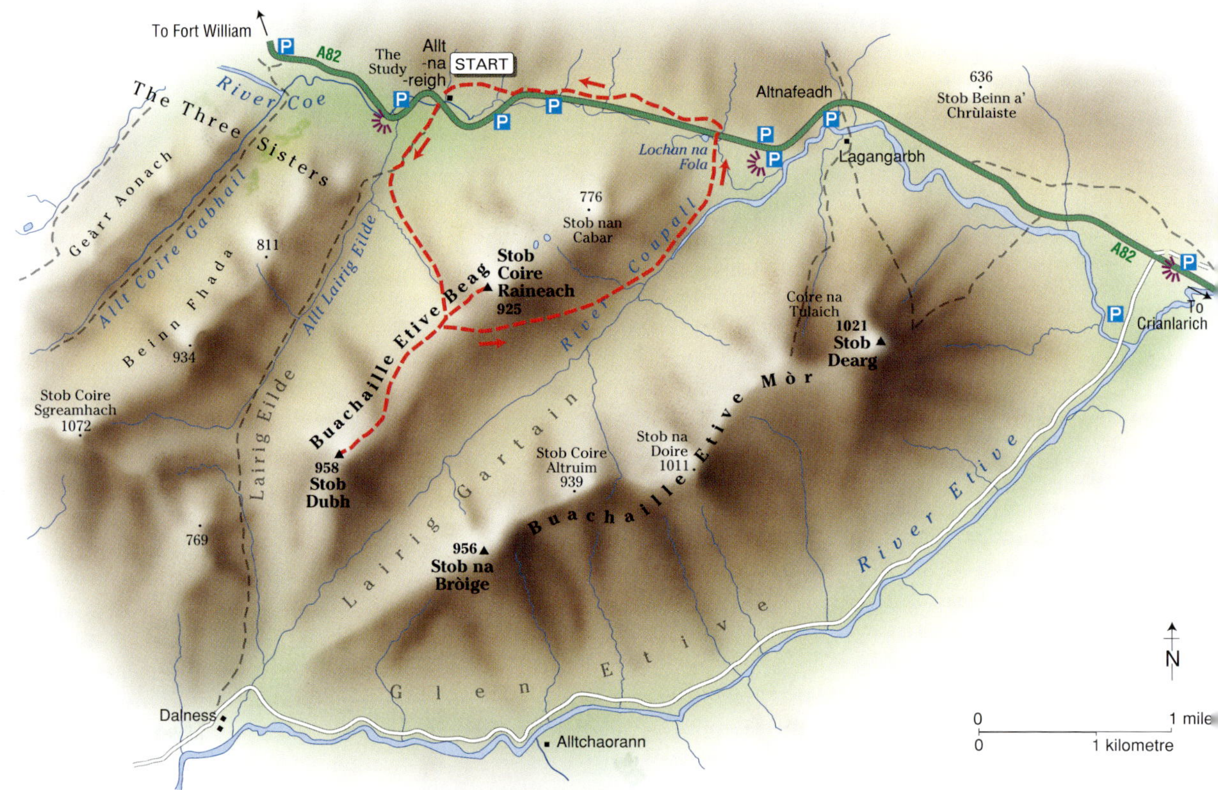

To Fort William
A82
The Study
Allt -na -reigh
START
River Coe
The Three Sisters
Gearr Aonach
Allt Coire Gabhail
Allt Lairig Eilde
Altnafeadh
636
Stob Beinn a' Chrùlaiste
Lochan na Fola
Lagangarbh
776
Stob nan Cabar
811
Beinn Fhada
934
Stob Coire Raineach
925
Buachaille Etive Beag
River Coupall
Coire na Tulaich
1021
Stob Dearg
To Crianlarich
Buachaille Etive Mòr
Stob Coire Sgreamhach
1072
Lairig Eilde
958
Stob Dubh
Stob na Doire
1011
Stob Coire Altruim
939
Lairig Gartain
769
956
Stob na Bròige
River Etive
Glen Etive
Dalness
Alltchaorann
N
0
1 mile
0
1 kilometre

4. Buachaille Etive Beag

Buachaille Etive Beag (the little herdsman of Etive) is a long wedge of a hill running between the head of Glen Coe and Glen Etive. Lying between Buachaille Etive Mòr and Bidean nam Bian it's a fine viewpoint for both hills. From the A82 road it's overshadowed by the massive north face of Buachaille Etive Mòr as, unlike that peak, the highest point lies at the south-west end of the hill overlooking Glen Etive. From the latter glen it looks superb, Stob Dubh being a fine symmetrical cone matching that of Stob na Bròige at the south-western end of Buachaille Etive Mòr with the U-shaped glaciated valley of the Lairig Gartain between them. There are two Munros on Buachaille Etive Beag – 958m Stob Dubh (black peak) and 925m Stob Coire Raineach (peak of the corrie of bracken). The walking is easy on Buachaille Etive Beag and the traverse of the ridge has excellent views throughout.

The walk starts just east of The Study, where the Allt Lairig Eilde plunges into the River Coe in a fine

A good ridge walk with fine views of Glen Etive and the surrounding hills. Mostly on paths but some pathless sections where good route finding skills are required. The paths in the glens can be very boggy.

BUACHAILLE ETIVE BEAG:

Stob Coire Raineach *(263), 925m/3035ft stop kora ran-ach; peak of the corrie of bracken*

Stob Dubh *(201), 958m/3143ft stop doo; black peak*

Start/Finish
Car park at start of Lairig Eilde path east of The Study / Altnafeadh car park

Distance
12km (7.5 miles)

Ascent
985m (3166ft)

Time *4–5 hours*

Difficulty ★

Maps *Harvey British Mountain Map Ben Nevis & Glen Coe, Harvey Superwalker Glen Coe, OS Explorer 384, OS Landranger 41*

Public Transport
Scottish Citylink buses run through Glen Coe

Facilities *Kings House Hotel*

Stob nan Cabar (the peak of the rafters), the northernmost summit of Buachaille Etive Beag, is steep and rocky and can be climbed by a scramble. Walking routes bypass this summit.

waterfall. The Study itself is a flat-topped rock some 30m above the A82 beside the old road. The classic romantic view of Glen Coe is from The Study, looking down the glen with the massive buttresses of the Three Sisters on the left and the jagged ridge of the Aonach Eagach on the right.

There are parking places on the A82 near The Study. A few hundred metres to the east a Scotways signpost indicates the public footpath to the Lairig Eilde. Follow this path some 750m to a junction shortly before a ford of the Allt Lairig Eilde. Take the left fork here (the right fork continues up to the Lairig Eilde then descends to Glen Etive) and follow the path as it makes a climbing traverse across the slopes of Stob Coire Raineach to the saddle south-west of the summit. Turn left on the ridge and ascend the short distance to the top, from where there are excellent views of the Glen Coe peaks.

Return to the saddle and continue south-west over a subsidiary top to Stob Dubh and another good view, this time of the Glen Etive hills. Stob Coire Sgrèamhach on Bidean nam Bian also looks impressive from here. The best view is a little further on than the summit. The south ridge of the mountain plunges steeply down to Glen Etive, an arduous ascent and knee-jarring descent. Although you could go down this way and return via the Lairig Eilde it's easier to retrace your steps to the saddle again then cut downwards and eastwards across the pathless slopes of Stob Coire Raineach to join the Lairig Gartain path beside the River Coupall. Follow this boggy path to a ford of the burn running out of Lochan na Fola and the A82. Rather than walk along the high-speed road cross it to the old road on the far side, which can be taken back to The Study.

Stob Dubh, Buachaille Etive Beag. Stob Dubh is the taller of Buachaille Etive Beag's two Munros, the second, Stob Coire Raineach, was only give full Munro status in 1997.

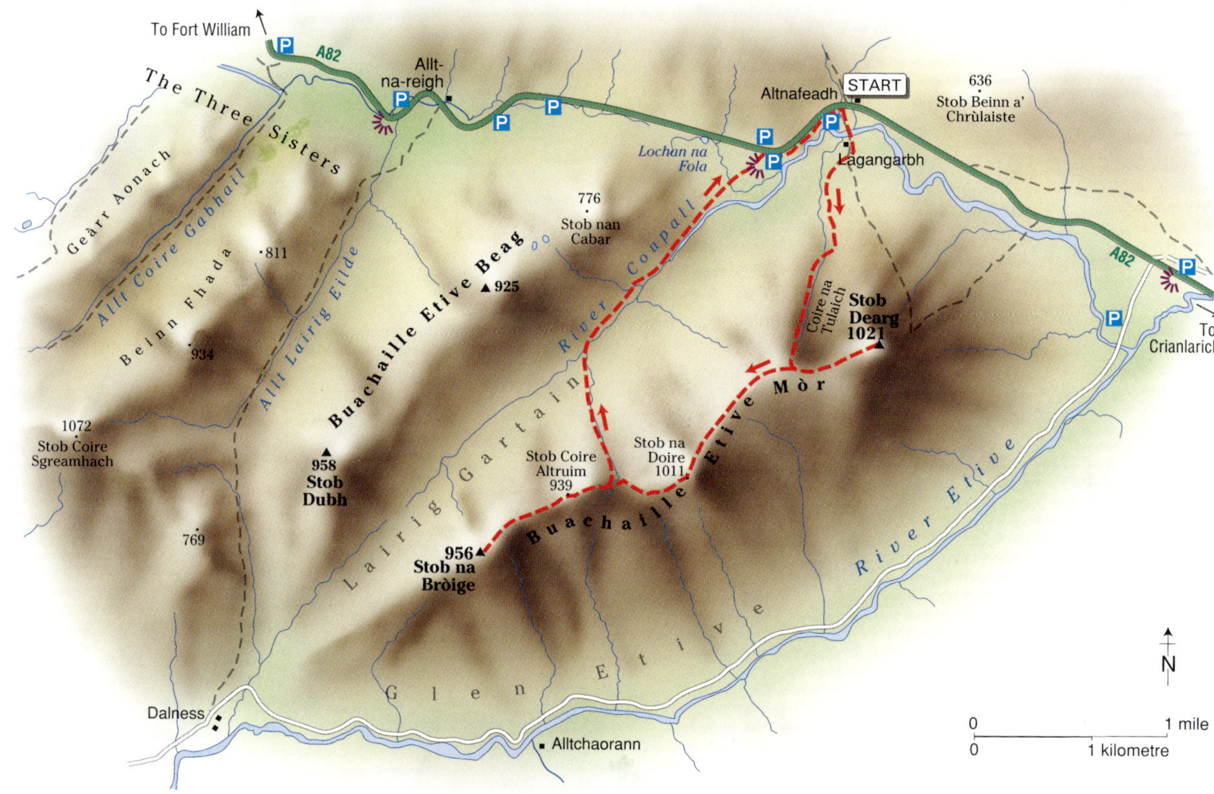
To Fort William
A82
Allt-na-reigh
START
Altnafeadh
636
Stob Beinn a' Chrùlaiste
The Three Sisters
Lochan na Fola
Lagangarbh
Gearr Aonach
Allt Coire Gabhail
776
Stob nan Cabar
811
Beinn Fhada
Allt Lairig Eilde
Buachaille Etive Beag
925
River Coupall
Coire na Tulaich
Stob Dearg 1021
934
A82
To Crianlarich
Mòr
1072
Stob Coire Sgreamhach
958 Stob Dubh
Lairig Gartain
Stob Coire Altruim 939
Stob na Doire 1011
Buachaille Etive
River Etive
769
956 Stob na Bròige
Glen Etive
N
0
1 mile
0
1 kilometre
Dalness
Alltchaorann

5. Buachaille Etive Mòr

Buachaille Etive Mòr (the great herdsman of Etive) is an iconic Highland mountain, a magnificent great rock pyramid rising out of the bogs of Rannoch Moor. Its position on the edge of the moor means it stands out in views from the A82 road, which runs past its foot before descending into Glen Coe. The mountain walls upper Glen Etive and runs parallel to its little brother to the west, Buachaille Etive Beag. It's a long mountain, stretching some 7.5km end to end. The summit ridge runs south-west to north-east for 4km over four summits, two of which – 1021m Stob Dearg (red peak) at the north end and 956m Stob na Bròige (peak of the shoe) at the south end – are Munros. Buachaille Etive Mòr is steep on all sides with big cliffs on its north-east face that harbour some of the most famous and challenging rock climbs in the Highlands. For walkers the traverse of the mountain is a rough walk, much of it over scree and rock.

The walk starts at Altnafeadh on the A82 north of

A big, rough walk over steep, loose and rocky terrain. Route finding can be awkward in mist. Some sections are slippery when wet. In winter snow can make this route dangerous. Splendid views of Rannoch Moor & Glen Etive.

BUACHAILLE ETIVE MÒR:

Stob Dearg *(110), 1021m/3350ft stop jerrack; red peak*

Stob na Bròige *(207), 956m/3136ft stop na broo-ka; peak of the shoe*

Start/Finish *Altnafeadh*

Distance *14km (8.5 miles)*

Ascent *1250m (4017ft)*

Time *6-8 hours*

Difficulty ★★

Maps *Harvey British Mountain Map Ben Nevis & Glen Coe, Harvey Superwalker Glen Coe, OS Explorer 384, OS Landranger 41*

Public Transport *Scottish Citylink buses run through Glen Coe*

Facilities *Kings House Hotel, The Clachaig Inn, Glen Coe NTS Visitor Centre, Glencoe village*

the mountain where there is room for parking. Follow a track south a short distance to a bridge over the River Coupall. Across the bridge a good path runs past white-washed Lagangarbh, a climbing hut belonging to the Scottish Mountaineering Club. Ahead rises the massive north face of Stob Dearg. A hundred metres or so beyond Lagangarbh the path forks. Take the right branch that heads across flat boggy moorland then climbs into wild, rocky Coire na Tulaich, the only break in the rock buttresses of the north face. There is some easy scrambling on the ascent of this corrie. In winter snow can build up with cornices on the rim and avalanches sometimes sweep the corrie.

The most arduous part of the walk comes next as the path climbs steep scree and rocks on the right-hand side of the corrie. The corrie becomes narrower and steeper at the top where a narrow loose gully runs up to the summit ridge. The path takes to a little rocky rib beside this gully for a final delightful little scramble before arriving on a broad, stony saddle from where myriads of cairns lead east over boulders for 700m and 150m of ascent to Stob Dearg, the highest point of Buachaille Etive Mòr.

The big summit cairn is right on the edge of the cliffs of the east face and there's a wonderful view east over the flat pool and stream flecked vastness of Rannoch Moor to far off hills. To the south-west the broad ridge of Buachaille Etive Mòr stretches out to Stob na Bròige. Follow the cairns back to the saddle at the head of Coire na Tulaich then continue along the ridge east over an unnamed 902m top then south-west to a fairly steep climb to 1011m subsidiary peak Stob na Doire (peak of the copse), another fine viewpoint. Take care when leaving this peak to turn right and take the path running south-west and not the one running south, which leads onto steep, dangerous terrain above Glen Etive. The descent from Stob na Doire leads to the lowest point on the ridge at 810m, which is the saddle between Stob na Doire and the next subsidiary peak 939m Stob

Looking south-west to Stob na Bròige from Stob na Doire on Buachaille Etive Mòr (the great herdsman of Etive).

Stob Dearg from the north-west (left).

A view along the ridge to Stob Dearg from Stob na Broige.

Stob Dearg, Buachaille Etive Mòr. The great rock pyramid of 'the Buachaille' rises out of the bogs of Rannoch Moor, and prevails as one of Scotland's iconic mountains (right).

Coire Altruim. Just above the saddle on the ascent of the last peak a small cairn marks the start of a path down into Coire Altruim, which is the descent route. First though follow a kink in the south-west trending ridge and climb just north of west to Stob Coire Altruim (peak of the nursing – of deer calves). Turning back south-west on the summit descend slightly then climb gently to Stob na Bròige from where there is an excellent view straight down Glen Etive to Loch Etive set between steep peaks. From Stob na Bròige return over Stob Coire Altruim to the start of the path into Coire Altruim. This path is steep, loose and badly eroded at the top and lower down a little easy scrambling is needed down some slabs before a better path runs through grass and bog to the River Coupall and the Lairig Gartain. Ford the little river to join a muddy path that runs down the wide, boggy glen to the A82 about 800m west of Altnafeadh.

Buachaille Etive Mòr can be combined with Buachaille Etive Beag for a long but rewarding day by either descending steeply north-west from Stob na Bròige to the top of the Lairig Gartain then climbing equally steeply up Stob Dubh or by descending the long south-west ridge of Stob na Bròige to Glen Etive then climbing the equally long south ridge of Stob Dubh.

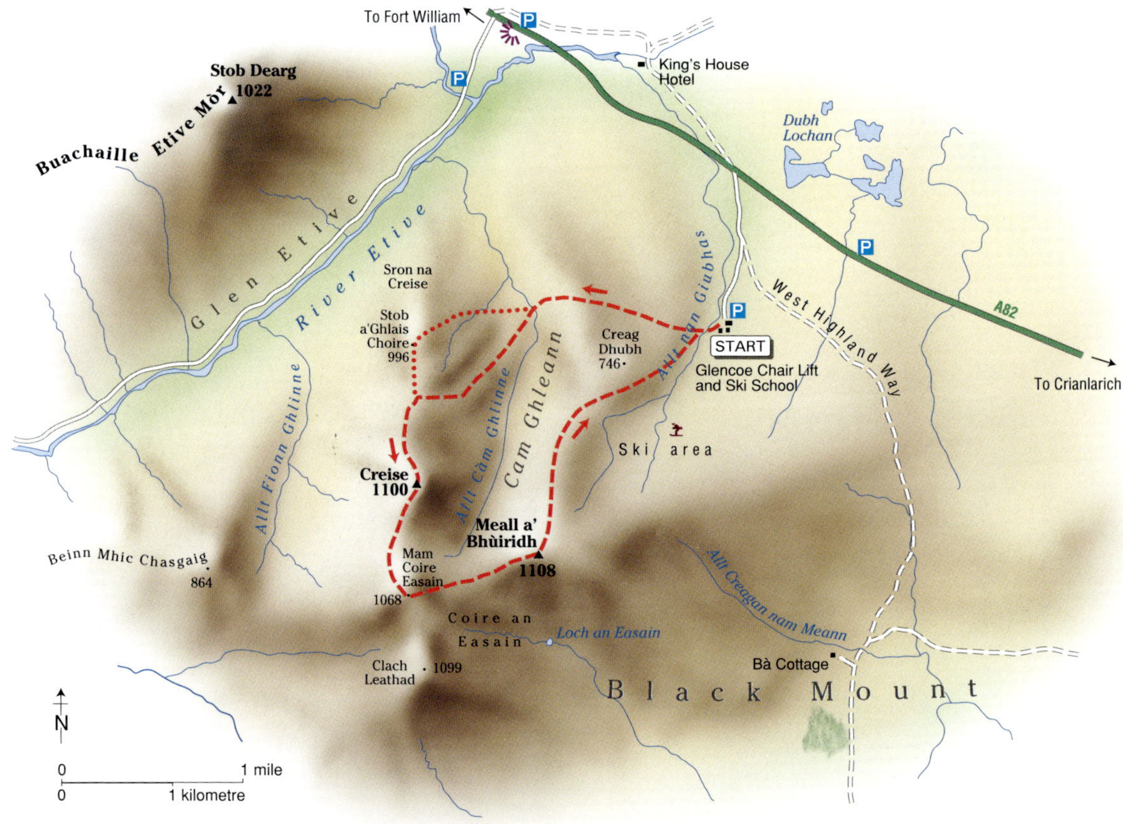

To Fort William
P
King's House Hotel
Stob Dearg
1022
Buachaille Etive Mòr
Dubh Lochan
Glen Etive
River Etive
P
Sron na Creise
Stob a'Ghlais Choire
996
Cam Ghleann
Creag Dhubh
746
Allt nan Giubhas
START
Glencoe Chair Lift and Ski School
West Highland Way
A82
To Crianlarich
Allt Cam Ghlinne
Allt Fionn Ghlinne
Ski area
Creise
1100
Meall a' Bhùiridh
1108
Beinn Mhic Chasgaig
864
Mam Coire Easain
1068
Coire an Easain
Loch an Easain
Allt Creagan nam Meann
Bà Cottage
Clach Leathad
1099
Black Mount
N
0
1 mile
0
1 kilometre

6. The Northern Black Mount

The great range of hills known as the Black Mount (a direct translation of the Gaelic, An Monadh Dubh) rises abruptly on the western edge of Rannoch Moor, separating the flat moor from Glen Etive. At the northern end of this range a steep rocky horseshoe curves round the long corrie of the Cam Ghleann. There are two Munros on this horseshoe – 1100m Creise (probably meaning narrow) and 1108m Meall a'Bhùiridh (hill of the roaring – of rutting red deer stags).

These hills look impressive from upper Glen Etive and from the A82 road across Rannoch Moor. The latter harbours the Glencoe Mountain Resort (formerly the White Corries Ski Resort) on its north-eastern flanks and it's from the resort that this circuit of the horseshoe starts (there is an alternative start about a km down the Glen Etive road from the A82 but this involves a ford of the River Etive, which may be dangerous or impossible after rain). The sides of

A steep rough circuit with narrow arêtes and potential route finding difficulties. A serious mountaineering proposition in winter. Wonderful views of Rannoch Moor.

THE NORTHERN BLACK MOUNT:

Creise *(50), 1100m/3609ft kraysh; narrow*

Meall a'Bhùiridh *(45), 1108m/3635ft mowl a vooree; hill of the roaring – of rutting red deer stags*

Start/Finish *Glencoe Mountain Resort*

Distance *10km (6 miles)*

Ascent *1100m (3535ft)*

Time *5–6 hours*

Difficulty ★★

Maps *Harvey British Mountain Map Ben Nevis & Glen Coe, Harvey Superwalker Glen Coe, OS Explorer 384, OS Landranger 41, OS Landranger 50*

Public Transport *Scottish Citylink buses run along the A82*

Facilities *Kings House Hotel, Glencoe Mountain Resort (café)*

Meall a'Bhuiridh and Sron na Creise rise on the western edge of Rannoch Moor, seen here from near the Kings House Hotel. Originally built for cattle drovers in the 1740s, the hotel has been popular with hillwalkers and climbers for many years.

these hills are steep and rocky with some optional scrambling but the high summit ridges are fairly flat with easy going.

From the resort head west-north-west across the boggy moor below the steep prow of Creag Dubh to the Allt Cam Ghlinne at the mouth of the Cam Ghleann, a distance of around 2.25km. There are now two options. The hardest way is to cross the burn and climb the rocky north ridge of Sron na Creise where some easy scrambling is required. The easier way is to go up beside the burn for around a km then climb the north-east ridge of Stob a'Ghlais Choire. Both ascents are steep but no scrambling is required on the latter. If climbing Sron na Creise, there is an easy walk from the summit to Stob a'Ghlais Choire. The bouldery ridge narrows south of the last peak but the walking is still easy to Creise and the surroundings are superb, with deep corries either side and the symmetrical red rock pyramid of Meall a'Bhùiridh rising across the depths of the Cam Ghleann.

From Creise the now grassy ridge continues south to a barely noticeable 1068m minor top called Mam Coire Easain (not named on most maps). A cairn here marks the start of a spur that runs out to Meall a'Bhùiridh. The ridge is quite featureless here and continues on without much elevation change for one km to another top called Clach Leathad so it's important to locate the cairn. The whole ridge stretches 3km in an almost straight line from Sron na Creise to Clach Leathad.

The complex topography of the Black Mount hills, a mass of ridges and corries, is revealed in this view south from Meall a'Bhùiridh to Stob Ghabhar across the ridge of Sron nam Forsair.

From Mam Coire Easain descend steeply east over granite boulders down the narrow rocky spur to the little 930m saddle separating the Cam Ghleann, in which the Allt Cam Ghlinne runs in a deep ravine, to the north and Coire an Easain to the south-east. The situation is dramatic with splendid

Meall a'Bhùiridh from Clach Leathad with the wilds of Rannoch Moor to the east beyond.

views down into the wild corries either side but there are no difficulties on the descent. Above the saddle rises the broader rocky west ridge of Meall a'Bhùiridh. Climb this to the stony summit, the highest point on the Black Mount and a wonderful viewpoint for Rannoch Moor, whose flat watery expanse stretches away into the eastern distance. Back west the long flat-topped, steep-sided ridge of Creise stretches out. More impressive than Creise itself is the more defined and pointed peak of one metre lower Clach Leathad (stone slope), which used to be the Munro until Creise was found to be that little bit higher.

The highest ski machinery of the resort lies just below the summit of Meall a'Bhùiridh, but this shouldn't ruin the wild feel of the mountain. You could descend back to the resort buildings through the ski runs, but this would be a poor way to end a fine day's walk. Better to go down the broad north ridge of the mountain almost to Creag Dhubh only then turning east down to the ski tows and a final descent. If you have started from Glen Etive continue on to Creag Dhubh and descend the north-west ridge then cross the moor to the glen.

The Bridge of Orchy hills from Meall a'Bhùiridh (right).

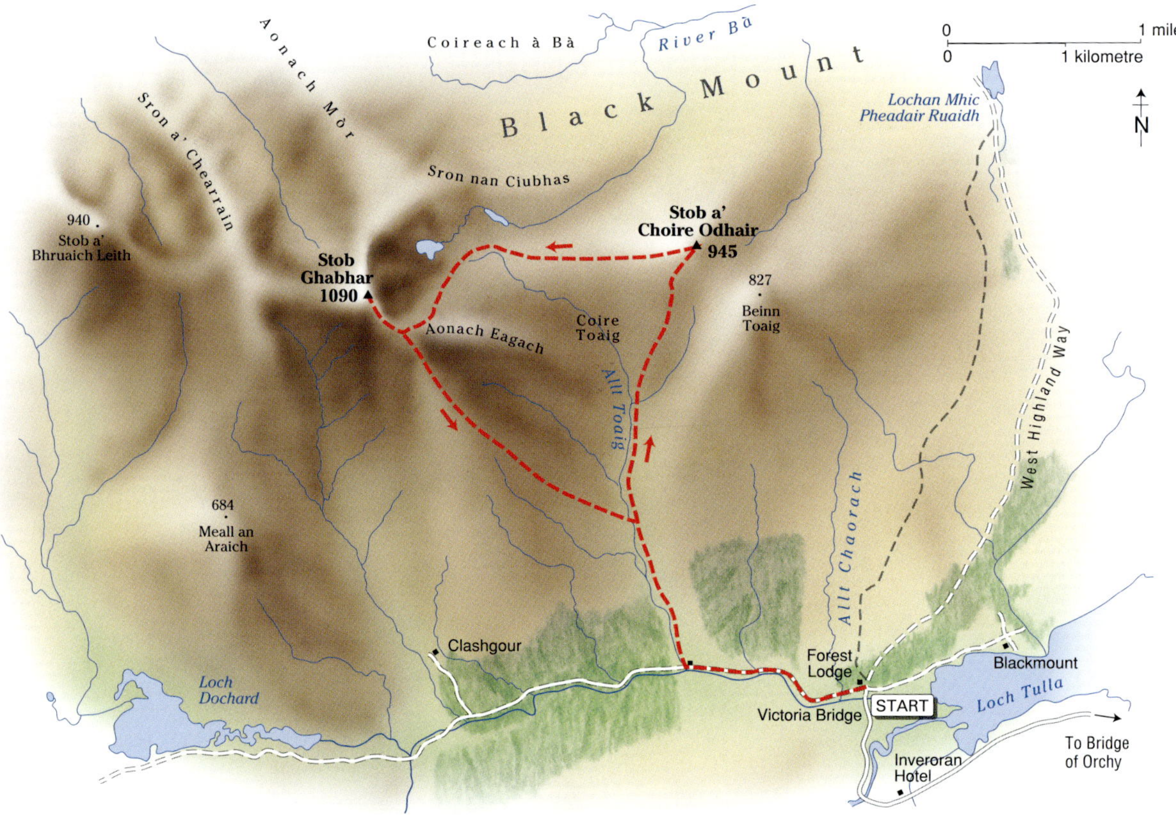

Coireach à Bà
River Bà
Black Mount
Aonach Mòr
Sron a' Chearrain
Sron nan Ciubhas
0
1 mile
0
1 kilometre
N
Lochan Mhic
Pheadair Ruaidh
940
Stob a'
Bhruaich Leith
Stob a'
Choire Odhair
945
Stob
Ghabhar
1090
827
Beinn
Toaig
Coire
Toaig
Aonach Eagach
Allt Toaig
West Highland Way
Allt Chaorach
684
Meall an
Araich
Clashgour
Forest
Lodge
Blackmount
Loch
Dochard
START
Loch Tulla
Victoria Bridge
Inveroran
Hotel
To Bridge
of Orchy

7. The Southern Black Mount

The southern Black Mount is a complex tangle of ridges radiating out from the highest peak, 1090m Stob Ghabhar (peak of the goats). The east ridge of this peak runs out to the second Munro in the group, 945m Stob a' Choire Odhair (peak of the dun-coloured corrie). Because it is the first big peak rising above Rannoch Moor Stob a' Choire Odhair stands out in views from the A82 road as it rounds Loch Tulla. Stob Ghabhar becomes more dominant as you progress along the minor road from Bridge of Orchy to the Inveroran Hotel and Victoria Bridge, where the round of the two Munros begins. Both are steep, rocky hills and the ascent of them makes for a tough walk. There are no difficulties though in poor visibility careful route finding is required in places.

Cross Victoria Bridge towards Forest Lodge then take the track left (west) beside the Abhainn Shira and follow this for 1.5km to a small corrugated iron hut near the Allt Toaig where a path branches off

A steep, rocky walk in complex terrain. Good route finding skills are needed. Challenging in winter conditions. Excellent views of Rannoch Moor and the Northern Black Mount.

THE SOUTHERN BLACK MOUNT:

Stob Ghabhar *(55), 1090m/3576ft stop gower; peak of the goats*

Stob a' Choire Odhair *(226), 945m /3100ft stob a kora ooer; peak of the dun-coloured corrie*

Start/Finish
Victoria Bridge

Distance
16km (10 miles)

Ascent
1275m (4098ft)

Time *6–8 hours*

Difficulty ★★

Maps *Harvey British Mountain Map Ben Nevis & Glen Coe, Harvey Superwalker Glen Coe, OS Explorer 384, OS Landranger 41, OS Landranger 50*

Public Transport
Scottish Citylink buses run through Bridge of Orchy, railway station at Bridge of Orchy

Facilities
Inveroran Hotel, Bridge of Orchy

Stob Ghabhar, seen here from Stob a' Choire Odhair, is a complex hill with six ridges and eight big corries.

northwards. Follow this path up beside the attractive tumbling burn for 2km with increasingly rugged slopes closing in on either side. Where the path crosses a side stream at GR 253446 leave it, just before it turns north-west, and continue north up the broad south ridge of Stob a' Choire Odhair on the zigzags of an old, well-constructed, stalker's path. This path peters out as the boulder-strewn slope eases at 750m. Continue on over the stones of a widening plateau to the summit and a splendid view north-east over Rannoch Moor with the chain of lochs along the Abhainn Ba prominent.

Turn away from the view of Rannoch Moor and face the massive east face of Stob Ghabhar, enclosed by the long arms of Sron nan Giubhas and the Aonach Eagach. The terrain is steep, rocky and complex and there is no obvious route to the summit. Luckily the climb is easier than it appears. Head down the broad west ridge of Stob a' Choire Odhair to the 668m saddle with Stob Ghabhar. From the saddle a rather indistinct little spur (clearer on the map than on the ground) curves round the head of Coire Toaig to the Aonach

Eagach. Climb this spur, at first heading west and then south. The going is through boulders and very rough and steep. Once on the Aonach Eagach turn west along the ridge, which is quite narrow and feels a touch exposed at one point, to the south-east ridge of Stob Ghabhar and follow this north-west to the rocky summit. Although higher Stob Ghabhar is not as good a viewpoint as Stob a' Choire Odhair as it lacks the extensive views of Rannoch Moor. However the immediate surroundings are more dramatic with big drops into dark corries and rocky ridges running away in every direction. Descend the stony south-east ridge of Stob Ghabhar to more open, grassy slopes at around 600m. Continue south-east to the Allt Toaig. Cross this to rejoin the path on the left bank and follow the outward route back to Victoria Bridge.

An alternative route up Stob Ghabhar runs from Alltchaorunn in Glen Etive along the long Aonach Mòr ridge, with a descent down Sron a'Ghearrain to the Allt Coire a'Chaolain, a distance of 16km with 1285m of ascent. It's awkward to add Stob a' Choire Odhair to this walk though, as you have to go out and back to it, involving an extra 6.5km of distance and 740m of ascent.

Stob Ghabhar lies on the southern edge of the Black Mount hills and has good views south-west to the peaks above Glen Etive and the distant Cruachan hills.

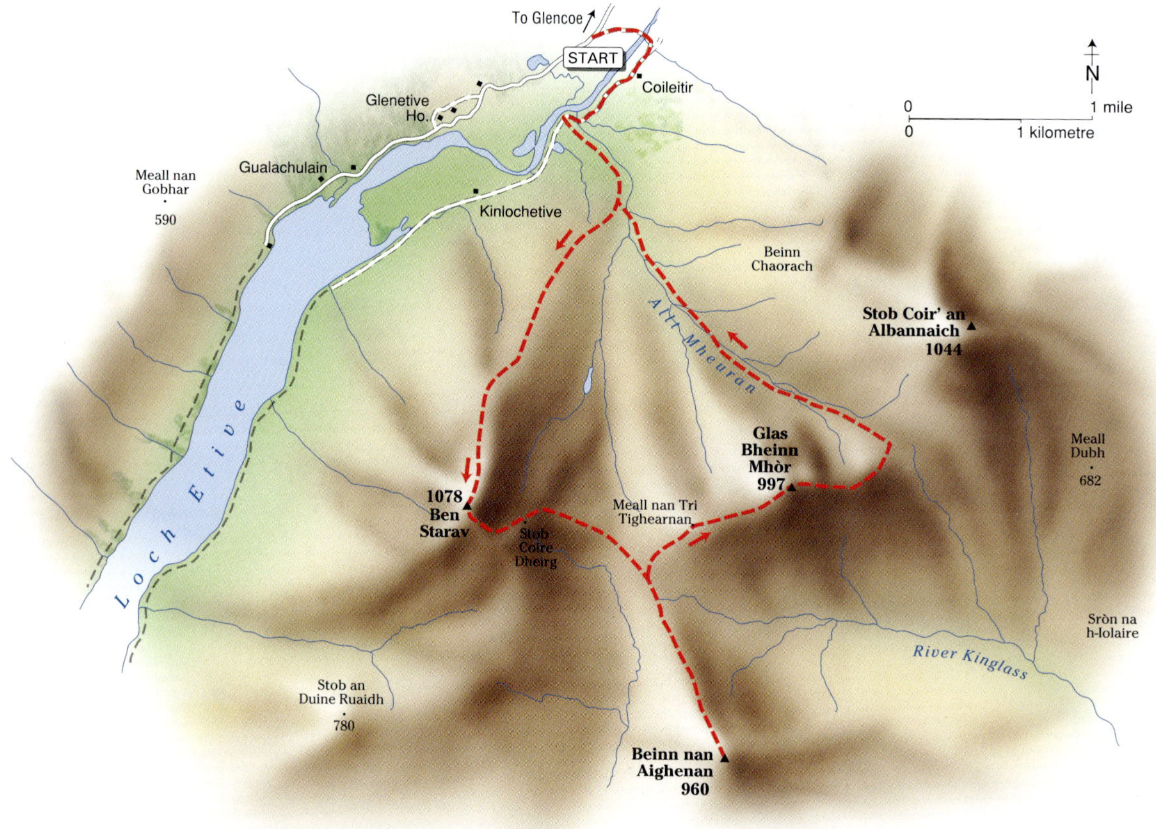
To Glencoe
START
Coileitir
N
0
1 mile
0
1 kilometre
Glenetive Ho.
Gualachulain
Meall nan Gobhar
590
Kinlochetive
Beinn Chaorach
Stob Coir' an Albannaich
1044
Allt Mheuran
Loch Etive
Glas Bheinn Mhòr
997
Meall Dubh
682
1078
Ben Starav
Stob Coire Dheirg
Meall nan Tri Tighearnan
Sròn na h-Iolaire
River Kinglass
Stob an Duine Ruaidh
780
Beinn nan Aighenan
960

8. Ben Starav, Beinn nan Aighenan & Glas Bheinn Mhòr

Rising steeply from Loch Etive, 1078m Ben Starav (meaning unknown – possibly hill of the rustling noise) is a spectacular mountain. Its massive rocky west face, seamed with gullies, looks particularly impressive from the hills on the far side of Loch Etive. The ascent of this Munro can be linked with two less distinctive but still worthy Munros – 960m Beinn nan Aighenan (hill of the hinds) and 997m Glas Bheinn Mhòr (big grey-green hill) – on a long, arduous but rewarding walk. Beinn nan Aighenan, one of the remotest hills in the Western Highlands, can be omitted to shorten the route by 4km and 600m of ascent.

The route starts on the minor road in lower Glen Etive at GR 137468 where a track runs down to a bridge over the River Etive, here running in an attractive rocky, tree-fringed gorge. Cross the bridge and turn right, following a track past the house of Coileitir to another bridge, this time over the Allt

Steep, rough and tough with some difficult navigation in poor visibility. Requires care in winter conditions. Some of the finest views in the Western Highlands from Ben Starav, especially down to Loch Etive.

Ben Starav *(63), 1078m/3537ft byn sta-rav; hill of the rustling noise*

Beinn nan Aighenan *(196), 960m/3150ft byn yan yanan;*

Glas Bheinn Mhòr *(145), 997m/3271ft glas vyn voar;*

Start/Finish
Lower Glen Etive

Distance
19.5km (12 miles)

Ascent
2000m (6428ft)

Time *8–10 hours*

Difficulty ★★★

Maps *Harvey British Mountain Map Ben Nevis & Glen Coe, Harvey Superwalker Glen Coe, OS Explorer 384, OS Landranger 50*

Public Transport
No public transport in Glen Etive

Facilities
The Clachaig Inn, Glen Coe NTS Visitor Centre, Glencoe village

The unrelenting north ridge of Ben Starav rises from sea level to the summit, a long though enjoyable ascent. From here at about 800m the majority of the climbing is over and your reward is near.

Mheuran, a stream again lined with pleasant mixed woodland. The path divides on the far side of this bridge. Follow the left fork uphill beside the burn for about half a km to the foot of the north ridge of Ben Starav, which rises straight to the summit. The ascent is steep but not difficult and there is a path the whole way. There are tremendous views down to Loch Etive and across to the dome of Glas Bheinn Mhòr. The ridge is quite broad except at the very top where it crosses granite boulders and scree. The summit of Ben Starav is a magnificent viewpoint, one of the very best in the Western Highlands. To appreciate it fully walk away from the cairn to the edge of the

steeper slopes. To the west there is a dizzying view down to Loch Etive at sea level. The loch runs away south, a deep trench between the hills, to the twin summits of Ben Cruachan. From south through east to north there is a splendid sweep of hills from Ben Lui to Bidean nam Bian.

The descent east from Ben Starav is awkward in poor visibility as the ridge twists and turns and there are side spurs that could lead you astray. Start by heading south-east for 400m to a bump at 1068m. Head north-east here, along a narrow rock arête with some avoidable easy scrambling, to the subsidiary top of 1027m Stob Coire Dheirg from where there is fine view back

The view from Ben Starav is extensive. Looking north brings a wonderful panorama of magnificent mountains: Bidean nam Bian, Buachaille Etive Mòr, Buachaille Etive Beag and the other Glen Coe peaks.

Looking south from Ben Starav to the hills of Argyll and the distinctive twin peaks of Ben Cruachan to the right.

to Ben Starav. From Stob Coire Dheirg descend more steeply east down a narrow stony ridge past rows of big rock pinnacles to a saddle at 767m below the minor top of Meall nan Tri Tighearnan. Traverse south-east across the slopes of the latter top to the saddle south of Beinn nan Aighenan and climb the rocky north ridge to the summit, from where you can look north-west back to Ben Starav and on north-east to Glas Bheinn Mhòr. Return to the 767m saddle and climb easily to Meall nan Tri Tighearnan. Turn right (east) here and continue on to the mossy summit of Glas Bheinn Mhòr. Ben Starav, Glen Etive and the hills south of Glen Coe look very fine from here.

There are steep crags to the north so a direct descent can't be made from Glas Bheinn Mhòr. Instead continue along the ridge east and then north-east to the saddle at the head of the Allt Mheuran glen. Keep right to avoid little crags on the final steep section above the saddle. Descend easily from the saddle into the boggy glen and follow the burn, on the left side of which a rough path soon appears, crossing to the right bank just before the confluence with the Allt Choire Dhuibh. Soon after the path fords the burn a fine waterfall is reached. This is the Eas nam Meirlach – the Robber's Waterfall. A chain of little cascades tumbles down rocky slopes then the main fall drops some 15m in a gloomy, narrow gorge. Continue on down the path to join the outward path beside the River Etive.

Looking east from Ben Starav to the rounded summit of Glas Bheinn Mhòr, where there are fine vistas of Glen Etive, the southern Glen Coe hills and countless inviting mountains to the east.

Walking in the Scottish Hills

Access & Responsibilities

There is a legal right of access to the hills in Scotland and so there is no need to worry about trespassing, obtaining permission or having to stay on paths. However, with access rights come responsibilities. For hill walkers these responsibilities fall into three categories. Firstly you should have respect for the land, which means leaving it as you find it and not doing any damage or leaving any litter. Secondly you should respect other people, both others using the hills for recreation and those who live and work in the hills, which means not interfering with their work, tools or buildings, not jeopardising their safety and allowing them privacy. Finally you are also responsible for your actions and your own safety. Full details of your rights and responsibilities and those of land managers can be found in the Scottish Outdoor Access Code, published as a book by Scottish Natural Heritage and available on the internet at www.outdooraccess-scotland.com.

Between July 1 and late-October is deer stalking season (though many estates don't start stalking until mid-August). During this period estates may request walkers to avoid certain routes or areas on days when stalking is taking place. Walkers should follow reasonable requests and avoid walking where stalking is taking place. Information on stalking may be posted on signs and notices at the start of paths. An increasing number of estates record messages for the Hillphones scheme, organised by Scottish Natural Heritage and the Mountaineering Council of Scotland, so you can ring and hear a recorded message giving advice about stalking. For more information see the Hillphones website – www.snh.org.uk/hillphones.

Terrain & Walking Times

Climbing Munros means dealing with a huge variety of terrain – forests, moorland, peat bogs, steep rocks, narrow ridges, broad plateaux and more. Paths and tracks are often used to approach the hills. However high in the hills paths may be narrow, sketchy or non-existent. Walking times are hard to estimate and involve more than distance and height ascended. The nature of the terrain is significant. Bogs, scree and boulders can slow you down. Even so, it is necessary to have an approximate idea of how long a walk will take. Back in 1892 Scottish mountaineer W. W. Naismith worked out a timings guide, known since as Naismith's Rule. This allows for an hour for every 3mi / 5km of distance and half an hour for every 1000ft / 300m of ascent. For the rough timings in this book I have used Naismith's Rule but also my own experience and the type of terrain.

Maps & Navigation

Navigation is an essential skill for climbing Munros. Although there are paths these can be faint or even non-existent in places and junctions are not signposted. When the mist closes in or snow covers the ground, navigation can be difficult and it is easy to go astray. Good skill with map and compass is essential then. The only adequate maps are the Harvey Maps 1:25,000 Superwalker and 1:40,000 British Mountain Maps, and Ordnance Survey 1:50,000 Landranger and 1:25,000 Explorer series. Digital versions of these maps can be found on CD and online from companies like Anquet and Memory Map so you can print out the area you need. Digital maps can also be used with handheld GPS units and Pocket PCs. A GPS is a great aid to navigation; though note that like a compass it tells you nothing about the terrain. The best compasses are baseplate or protractor models that can be used to take bearings off the map.

Safety & Equipment

Climbing the Munros is a safe activity if basic precautions are followed. Very few of the tens of thousands who climb Munros every year have accidents. The weather can be wet and windy and the terrain is often steep and rugged so good hillwalking equipment is needed. This should include hillwalking footwear, warm and waterproof clothing, torch, whistle, map, compass, first aid kit, survival bag or group shelter and rucksack. In winter conditions extra warm clothing and a warm hat and gloves are also needed. When snow and ice lie on the hills an ice axe and crampons and the skill to use them are essential. Winter weather can be severe and walkers should heed the weather forecast (the Mountain Weather Information Service is recommended – www.mwis.org.uk). Avalanches are a hazard in snowy conditions. The SportScotland Avalanche Information Service publishes daily avalanche forecasts (www.sais.gov.uk) from mid December to mid April that should be consulted if there's snow on the hills.

Whilst getting lost or having an accident is unlikely, these mishaps can happen. Leaving details of your route with a responsible person is advisable plus a time by which you will make contact to say you are back. Don't forget to let them know once you finish the walk, whenever it is, to avoid an unnecessary rescue call-out. If an incident occurs and you need help call 112 or 999 and ask for the police and then mountain rescue. Note that mobile phones do not receive signals everywhere in the hills. Someone may have to walk out some distance to call for help. Anyone calling mountain rescue should provide details of the location and the nature of the incident. Please support mountain rescue teams by donating via the collection boxes found in bars, cafes and outdoor shops in mountain areas. The teams are made up of volunteers and provide an invaluable service.

Advice to Readers

Walking and scrambling in the Scottish hills can be dangerous, and should only be undertaken by those who have prior competent knowledge of mountain safety, and who are physically capable, properly equipped and fully prepared for walking and climbing in the mountains. All walkers must rely on their own judgement and experience, and always walk safely within their own abilities. All maps are provided for illustrative purpose only. Please use the appropriate Harvey or Ordnance Survey maps for your walk. Colin Baxter Photography and its author accept no liability whatsoever for injury or damage caused to or by walkers, or to their property, or to third parties arising from the use of this walking guide. While great care has been taken to ensure the content of this book is accurate, no responsibility is accepted for any errors or ommissions.

Chris Townsend is a freelance author and photographer. His fifteen books include the award-winning *The Backpacker's Handbook* and *The Munros and Tops*, an account of his continuous round of all the 3000 foot summits in Scotland, the first time this walk had been done. Chris has also completed many long distance walks abroad including the Pacific Crest Trail and the first ever walk along the entire length of the Canadian Rockies. Chris writes for *TGO* magazine every month and his website is: **www.christownsendoutdoors.co.uk**.

Published in Great Britain in 2008 by
Colin Baxter Photography Ltd,
Grantown-on-Spey, Moray PH26 3NA, Scotland
www.colinbaxter.co.uk

Based on 1946 Ordnance Survey mapping with additional information from Harvey Maps and the Royal Commission on the Ancient and Historical Monuments of Scotland.

 A CIP Catalogue record for this book is available from the British Library.

ISBN 978-1-84107-408-5   Printed in China

Front cover: *Buachaille Etive Mòr.*
Page 1: *'The Three Sisters'.*   Page 2: *Glencoe from the air – looking east with Bidean nam Bian in the foreground.*